technology and you

Using the Internet Safely

By
Donna Loughran

RAINTREE
STECK-VAUGHN
RSVP PUBLISHERS

A Harcourt Company

Austin   New York
www.raintreesteckvaughn.com

Published by Raintree Steck-Vaughn Publishers, an imprint of Steck-Vaughn Company.

Library of Congress Cataloging-in-Publication Data is available upon request.

ISBN 0-7398-4697-3

Printed and bound in the United States.

1 2 3 4 5 6 7 8 9 0 WZ 07 06 05 04 03 02

Table of Contents

Chapter 1

Getting Connected

Have you heard about the Internet and wondered what it is all about? The Internet is all about connections. Two computers that are connected, for example, can share information. This ability to share information makes the two computers a network. The Internet is a worldwide network of computers hooked up to one another. In fact, it is a system of millions of connected computer networks around the world. These networks can take you almost any place on Earth. With the click of keys on a keyboard, you can plan a vacation, send a message to the other side of the world, or play a game with someone in Europe, all without leaving your chair.

The "Enter" command on your computer keyboard can be the gateway to the world of the Internet.

When most people think of the Internet, they think of the Web. Web is short for the World Wide Web. But the Web and the Internet are different.

The Internet is a system of computers and programs. It began in the early 1960s. The Web was born 30 years later. It is a program that makes it possible for web pages and websites to work on the Internet. When you use your computer to connect to the Internet and then to the Web, you are online. Being online means you are using the Internet.

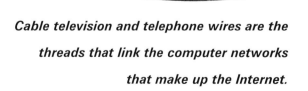

Cable television and telephone wires are the threads that link the computer networks that make up the Internet.

HARDWARE AND SOFTWARE

Besides a computer you will need a little machine called a modem. A modem is a machine that connects your computer to a phone or cable TV line. The modem changes information from your computer into a form that can be carried along phone or cable lines. Then, the modem brings information back from the Internet into your computer, changing it into a form your computer can understand. The modem might be in a box that sits on the desk next to your computer. A modem also might be a special card that fits inside your computer.

Techno Tip

Web pages are the pages you see on your computer screen when you connect to the Web. Many web pages linked together are called websites.

A modem is a device that connects your computer with cable television or telephone lines in order to receive data. The modem in this photograph makes use of a technology known as DSL (Digital Subscriber Line), which allows the transmission of a large amount of data at very high speeds.

You will also need a phone or cable socket, or connector, to plug the modem into. Your modem does not need to be plugged into your phone line when you are not using the Internet. But it does not matter if you leave it plugged in. It won't stop you from receiving phone calls or being able to watch TV shows. But when you are online your phone line is in use, so you will not be able to get any calls and no one will be able to use the phone.

A computer, a modem, and a phone or cable socket or connector are known as hardware. Hardware is the machinery you need to connect to the Internet.

To travel online, you also need software. Software is the name given to the programs that run on your computer. These programs are often called applications.

An "application" is a computer program designed to perform a specific task or function. Word processors, such as Word; web browsers, such as Explorer; and image editing programs, such as Photoshop, are all well-known examples of applications.

Some special applications allow you to connect to and travel to different places on the Internet and Web.

Before you can travel online, you need two things. First, you need an Internet Service Provider, or ISP. Second, you need a web browser.

No one owns the Internet, but you need an online service or ISP (Internet Service Provider) to connect to it. An ISP is a company that helps you connect to the Internet. Most ISPs charge users a monthly fee, although some are free. The ISP will help you to send and receive messages called electronic mail, or e-mail for short. The ISP will also let you download, or get, files off the Internet, like text, pictures, and music and video clips.

These days, a web browser can be found on many digital devices, including cellular phones.

Most ISPs open the door to the Internet, but they don't take you to the Web. To reach the Web, you need a special application, or tool, called a web

browser. What does it mean to browse? When you browse in a library, you look around at different books. A web browser is a software program that lets you look at different websites on the Internet. Browsing on the Internet or Web is also known as surfing.

In a library, a classification system makes it easier for readers to find books about similar topics. A web browser allows you to do much the same thing on the Internet.

Most computers come with a web browser already installed, or in place. You may know the names of two popular web browsers. One is Netscape Navigator. The other is Internet Explorer. They are alike in some ways and different in others. A web browser is like a ship that lets you travel online to places on the Web.

Before a web browser can rocket you to the Web, you must be connected to the Internet. Computers can be set up to do that automatically whenever you launch, or open, the web browser.

If you don't have a computer or Internet connection at home or at school, try your local public library. The people there will help you get "connected."

This technician is hooking up a server, which is a large computer that stores information for a system of interconnected computers, or network.

WHERE IS CYBERSPACE ANYWAY?

Now, you are almost ready to blast into cyberspace (pronounced sy-bur-space). What is cyberspace? Cyberspace is the name that some people give to the online "world." Cyberspace is the place you are when you hook your computer up to the Internet and meet other people through e-mail and chat and visit other computer "places," like websites.

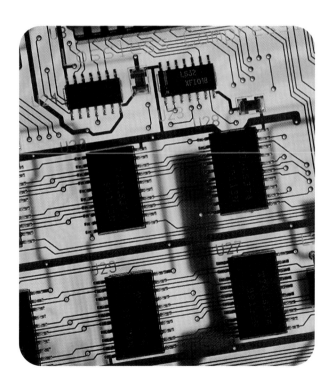

Although being online does not seem as real as visiting people face to face, or as real as visiting places with buildings and parks that you can touch and feel and smell, it is an easy way for people to meet "mind to mind," computer to computer, across great distances.

It's hard to believe that the relatively small number of chips, circuits, wires, and connectors found inside a personal computer can provide access to all of cyberspace.

BE A WISE CYBERTOURIST

Cyberspace is the name given to the place you are when you are online. But the Internet is actually more like a gigantic city than empty space. It is a cybercity made up of all types of people and places. In fact, you could call the Internet the largest city on Earth. In 2000, more than 400 million people from about 200 countries were on the Internet in just one month. Made up of citizens from around the world, the Internet cybercity is diverse and always changing.

Just like in any city, there are safe places to go and there are places that are not so safe. The best plan for someone visiting the Internet cybercity is to become "street smart" and learn what areas are safe, and what areas to avoid. What is being street smart? Some of you who live in cities may already know what this means.

Today, the Internet connects virtually the entire globe, and it continues to grow.

Being street smart means that you develop a kind of attitude that you put on and take with you into places that may be dangerous or even just unknown to you. This attitude means you are alert and on the defense. You keep your eyes and ears open for anything that might put you in a bad, dangerous, or negative situation. You are skeptical, meaning you don't believe everything you hear or see.

Techno Tip

Cybercrime (crime committed with the use of computers) has grown almost as fast as the Internet itself. Criminals use the Internet to commit everything from robbery to sex crimes.

The Internet, like any city, is made up of all types of people: the good, the bad, the smart, the not so smart, the misguided, the kind, and unfortunately, the not so kind. And then, there are the downright nasty people.

As many sorts of people as there are in the world, there are in the cybercity of the Internet. Think about it. Anyone who wants to can be online or can publish information on the Internet. That means that you have to develop your own filtering system to figure out what is safe and what is not. You may have to decide for yourself what is good for you and what is not.

Since there is no one governing body policing the cybercity, you have to put your street smarts on every time you use the Internet. Think of these street smarts as your "cybersmarts."

Everyone visiting a big city for the first time needs to make a plan. So do you. You need to know the safe areas of interest to visit and you need to know the places where you might get into trouble.

It is the same with the Internet. You need a guide to the cybercity to keep you on track and cybersurfing safely. Luckily, there are many people out there, both grownups and kids, who are ready to advise you on how to proceed on your visits to the cybercity.

The Internet allows you to pay a "virtual" visit to just about any city in the world.

Chapter 2

Putting Your Cybersmarts On!

Think of cybersmarts as a kind of protective hat or suit that you put on every time you sit down at the computer and go into the cybercity.

Do you remember when you were little, how you had to learn to look both ways before crossing the street? Or when your parents taught you about not talking to strangers around town? Traveling on the Web without knowing the safety rules for the Internet is like crossing the highway wearing a blindfold!

The Internet has been called an information superhighway. To travel it successfully, it helps to know the rules of the road and to have some idea of where you want to go.

Talk with your parents or guardians about what your home online-safety rules are. Here are some general rules you should also follow to be safe while you are online. You might want to call them the Cybersmarts Never Rules:

1. Never share your name, your phone number, or any personal information with anyone on the Internet.

2. Never tell anyone where you go to school, where you live, or any other details like school team names or school mascot names.

3. Never agree to get together with someone you meet online without first checking with your parents or guardians. If your parents agree to the meeting, make sure that your parents or guardians go with you and that the meeting is in a public place.

Be skeptical if anyone you "meet" online wants a lot of personal information, such as where you live, your phone number, or your parents' credit card numbers.

4. Never share pictures of yourself, your house, your family, or your friends. You have a responsibility to keep your friends and family safe, too!

5. Never send e-mail to people you don't know without checking it out with your family first.

6. Never tell a stranger your e-mail address. And, never, never tell anyone, even a friend, your computer or e-mail password.

7. Never respond to any messages that are mean or that make you feel uncomfortable. It is not your fault if you get a message like that. If someone says something that makes you feel unsafe or funny, don't just sit there—take charge! Tell your parents or guardians right away so that they can contact your online service or ISP.

8. Never accept or open e-mail or files from strangers!

9. Never go to a website that costs money unless you have your parents' permission.

Just as you lock your door when entering or leaving your house, to protect yourself, your family, and your possessions, you need to take steps to protect yourself in cyberspace.

Let your parents or guardians know what you are doing online. It is a good idea for the computer to be in a room that the whole family regularly uses. That way, all of your family can share the experience of going online.

There are also special software programs that filter, or keep out, negative places on the Web. SurfWatch is one of these filtering programs that is easy to use and that is available for Windows and Mac personal computers (PCs). America Online is an online service that monitors chat and e-mail in kids' areas on the Web. This service also lets your parents or guardians set limits on the areas of the Web that you can visit.

A parent or responsible adult should know what you are doing when you are online, just as they should be informed about all your activities.

Remember, always tell your parents or another adult you trust if you receive scary e-mail messages. The Internet is a wonderful place, but it also lets people hide what they really look like and the truth about themselves. So, it's really easy for weirdos to lie about who they are. Cybersmart kids don't believe what everyone says online.

So, put on your cybersmarts, fasten your cyber-safety belt, and get ready to blast off to visit the largest city on the planet, the Internet.

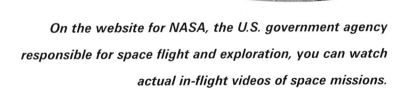

On the website for NASA, the U.S. government agency responsible for space flight and exploration, you can watch actual in-flight videos of space missions.

Chapter 3

Getting Ready to Travel Safely

When you're ready to launch yourself into the cybercity, make sure your modem is plugged into the phone or cable socket in the wall and that it is turned on. Then, start up your web browser. There might be a shortcut to it on the desktop of your computer screen. It will be an icon, or a little picture.

The icon might be found on the computer desktop's background or it might be on a button or toolbar. If you can't find it, you can open the browser from a menu. A menu is a window you open on your computer desktop. It lists different programs on your computer. If you are on a Windows PC, click the "Start" button and look in the "Programs" menu. If you're using a Mac PC, click on the

A few taps on a computer keyboard gains you access to the world of the Internet.

"Apple" menu and look around—you'll probably find your web browser listed in the "Recent Applications" or "Internet Access."

Your computer will dial your ISP's computer and after a short while you'll see your first web page. Congratulations! You are at the cybercity limits.

AT THE CYBERCITY LIMITS

A "Home page" is the first page or screen you see in your browser window after launching the browser program. It is the starting point of every journey in the cybercity. If you get lost, you can get back to it by clicking the Home icon on your browser window.

Usually, your computer comes with a home page in place. It is often the computer or the web browser's company website. You can leave the home page as it is or change it. A few simple clicks will change your home page to a page you choose.

Techno Tip

Ray Tomlinson created the first e-mail program. He was also the one that decided to use the "@" symbol as part of email addresses. The first message he sent was "QWERTYUIOP" which are the characters from the top row of letters on a standard keyboard.

Have a look at the browser window before you start to browse the Web. Whichever browser you are using, you'll need to know a bit about the browser window.

Look closely at the address line. Every web page has an address, or URL (Uniform Resource Locator in geek speak). This address tells the computer where to look for the page you want. So, just like an address on a letter it needs to be correct to be delivered. Let's take a closer look at the address:

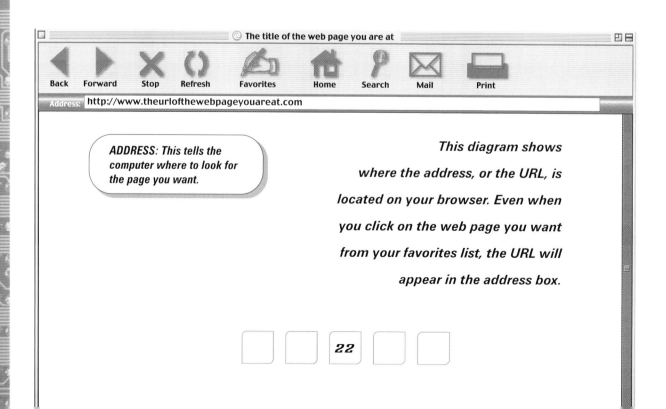

@ The title of the web page you are at

| Back | Forward | Stop | Refresh | Favorites | Home | Search | Mail | Print |

Address: http://www.theurlofthewebpageyouareat.com

ADDRESS: This tells the computer where to look for the page you want.

This diagram shows where the address, or the URL, is located on your browser. Even when you click on the web page you want from your favorites list, the URL will appear in the address box.

In a web address, www stands for the World Wide Web, but scientists are already planning to expand the web to other parts of our solar system. Some web addresses now end with a suffix that tells you the country of the organization that created the website. For example, .ca stands for Canada, .th for Thailand, and so on.

At some time in the near future, astronauts aboard the International Space Station may create and maintain their own website.

In the near future, space stations and computer stations orbiting other planets will have access to the web. That will mean that when you see web addresses that end with .sol , that particular website is literally out of this world!

MAKE A CYBERSMART SITE YOUR HOME PAGE

Okay, it's good to know where home is. It's like going away to camp with your name and address written in your underwear. You know you won't get lost.

But hold on! When kids visit a big city, they need a friend to show them around. The Internet has more people in it than any big city, so people need a friend to give them directions, there, too.

There are programs on the Web called search engines that can be a friendly guide for your visit. A search engine sounds like some kind of machine, but it's really just another kind of website—one that lets you search all the other millions of websites to find what you might be looking for in the cybercity. And, there are search engines built especially to be kid-friendly. These search engines can be your gateway, guide, and friend for the Web.

Techno Tip

Some search engines are "Crawler" based. They create their listings automatically. They "crawl" or search the website by site, then people search through what the search engine has found.

There are several cool search engines on the Web designed especially for kids. A librarian at school or at your public library, or a teacher in your school's computer lab, should be able to make some recommendations.

A portal is a gateway into the Web that points you to certain kinds of websites. Through a friendly search engine, or portal, you can find sites from around the world devoted to subjects such as entertainment, museums, science projects, homework help, and safe game sites that are only for kids.

Today, most libraries have someone who is trained to help you use the Internet as well as books for research and school projects.

These search engine websites act like a helpful guide, steering you to all the important sites of interest on the Web. These safe search engines can keep you clued into the newest, coolest, and most unusual sites in the cybercity. The best ones will also give you advice on being a safe cybersurfer.

Do you want to make a safe search engine that is designed especially for kids your home page? Here's how to do it. Type the address of the website you would like to be your home page into the address line in your browser window. In this example,

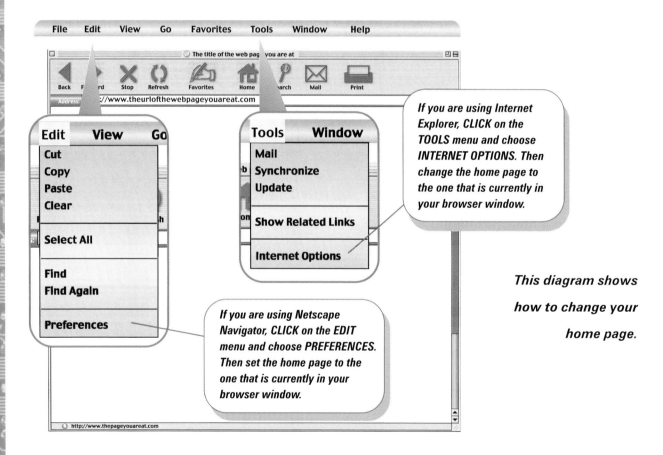

If you are using Internet Explorer, CLICK on the TOOLS menu and choose INTERNET OPTIONS. Then change the home page to the one that is currently in your browser window.

If you are using Netscape Navigator, CLICK on the EDIT menu and choose PREFERENCES. Then set the home page to the one that is currently in your browser window.

This diagram shows how to change your home page.

After it displays, do the following, depending on the web browser program you are using.

• If you are using Internet Explorer, open the "Tools" menu and choose "Internet Options." There's a button on the "General" tab to change your home page to the one that is currently shown in your web browser window.

• If you are using Netscape Communicator, open the "Edit" menu and choose "Preferences" to set the home page to the one that is currently shown in your web browser window.

Now, you are ready to step over the border into the cybercity. You are aware and alert. You know the Never Rules. You have your cybersmarts on, and you have your kid-friendly search engine as your home page to help you find what you want safely. Let's go explore!

Techno Tip

Sounds creepy, but spiders and bots are the names for tiny pieces of software that keep a search engine going. They spend their time crawling around the Web. They make a huge index, or list, of all that they find. When you ask the search engine to find something, it takes a quick look through the index and shows you what it finds.

Chapter 4

Exploring the Cybercity

There are three ways to use your search-engine home page. If you know the web address of the site you are interested in, type it into the address line in your web browser and hit the "return" key on your keyboard. This will take you directly to the site you want.

Or if you don't have an address, but you have a general subject in mind, you can click on a subject list that appears on your search-engine home page. These are hot links that will take you to an index of sites that relate to the subject you are interested in. You can tell the listed subjects are "hot," or are linked to other web pages, because they are usually underlined. Your onscreen mouse pointer, called a cursor, or the arrow you see onscreen when you move your mouse around, turns

Techno Tip

The World Wide Web is made up of more than a billion web pages linked together. You can follow a link from one page to another by clicking on it. A link might be words that are underlined and in a different color, buttons with words written on them, or small pictures called icons. Remember, you get a pointy finger cursor if you roll your mouse over something that is linked.

into a "pointy finger" when you roll it over a hot link. The pointy finger is a clue that something is hot and clickable.

Another way to use the search-engine home page is to type key words into the search box in the main body of the search engine page. Key words are words that represent the subject you are looking for. For example, if you are in need of homework help, you might type the key words homework+help into the search box and then hit the search button next to it. This key word search will open a hot list of homework websites that you can explore and choose from by clicking on each.

These days, children often teach parents or grandparents how to use the Internet.

A really great homework and research site is called KidsClick. The address is http://www.kidsclick.org/

Real-life librarians at the KidsClick site can help with every school subject since they know how and where to go to look up information about any subject. Check out all the subjects listed on the first page of the site. You can see that they are all hot links since they are underlined. Take some time to explore some of the different subjects listed here.

Where shall we go now? Let's jump back to your home page and your safe search engine by clicking the home icon in the browser window. Do you want to explore what it's like to be president? Do you want to go to a game site? Visit the pyramids in Egypt? Write world leaders? Since we are in a city, let's go visit a web museum.

You may not have the time or money to visit the pyramids in Egypt, but the Internet makes an online visit easy.

Type into the address box in your browser, http://www.exploratorium.edu/ and hit "return." If you want to see some cool stuff, go to this site. It includes online science museum exhibits with sounds, music, and all kinds of activities and games. You can do research here, have fun, jump to other science sites. Put this on your hot list. You'll want to keep coming back to this one.

As you surf, you will find sites you want to visit again. Browsers let you save your favorite sites. Go to the menu at the top of your screen. Your browser may say Bookmarks or Favorites. Click on the word. Click again on Add. Browsers make returning to your favorite sites easy. Click on Bookmarks or Favorites and choose the site you want to visit from the list.

The world's greatest paintings hang in museums and private collections around the world, but you can see many of them by using the Internet.

Have you ever wanted to understand how maps work? Would you like to learn how to use a compass? Try typing this address into your web browser address line: http://www.usgs.gov/education/ . This is the United States Geological Survey site for kids. Take a look at Map Wizard at this site to learn how to plot longitude and latitude. There are lots of other great activities here as well as clip art you can copy, or download, to your computer.

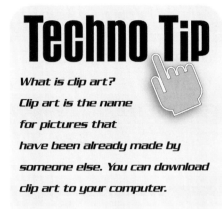

Techno Tip

What is clip art?
Clip art is the name
for pictures that
have been already made by
someone else. You can download
clip art to your computer.

Or, go to the CIA's (Central Intelligence Agency) site http://www.odci.gov/cia/publications/factbook/. The Factbook gives you up-to-date information about, and maps of, any place in the world. Every country and many regions are listed. For each country there's a ton of information, such as the country's location, land area, imports and exports, form of government, land use, population, and much more! You can download the maps here also.

Remember, to download just means that you are copying an image or file to your computer. If you find some art you would like to have, put your mouse cursor on the picture and click. A menu will appear. Choose "save this image as . . ." from the list in the menu and then save the image to a special folder or put it on your computer desktop for later use. You may want to save this image to include in a school report or send in an e-mail to a friend.

You can download images like this one, of elephants grazing on the African savannah, from the Internet to your personal computer.

If you want to make your computer laugh, cry, sneeze, or croak like a frog, travel to a sound-effects or music website. There, you can download any free sounds. Then you can use them on your computer or send them to a friend.

Even if you don't want to save the sounds to your computer, it's fun to click on the different sound effects, just to hear what they are.

To find some great sound effect sites, go back to your kid-friendly search engine and type the words sound+effects in the search box and hit the "search" button. A list of sound effect sites for you to explore will pop up.

The portraits of famous Americans in the National Portrait Gallery in Washington, D.C., can be viewed online.

No visit to a city is complete without a visit to an art museum. If you like art of any kind, you must stop off at http://www.ibiblio.org/louvre/. You'll find hundreds of the finest paintings and sculptures in the world there. You can get information about artists and art history.

As you browse the galleries and read, you also see tiny pictures of the art, or thumbnails. To see any painting full-screen, just click on the thumbnail picture and it will expand.

You can save any painting at this site to your own computer to print out or view at any time. You can also take a guided tour of Paris, France, at this site! Bon voyage!

For some fun game sites, you can click on the hot link on your search-engine home page listed 'games.'

Before we move on to more fun things to do in the cybercity of the Internet, take a look at the FBI's Internet Safety Site for kids—
www.fbi.gov/kids/crimepre/internet/internet.htm.

Techno Tip

To download or not? You can get drawings, cartoons, photos, animations, and even video clips off the Web. Usually you can have them without permission if you are not planning to resell them. Check to see if there is a note on the site next to the art that says how you can use the art.

Chapter 5

Using Cybermail

Keep your cybersmarts on when e-mailing. E-mail seems private, but there are people out there who know how to find out information about you through your e-mail, too!

E-mail is a message sent to someone's electronic mailbox, like sending a regular letter, only through cyberspace. E-mail, or electronic mail, is a smart way to send messages to other people you know who use the Internet and have e-mail accounts.

Internet users sometimes refer to regular mail as "snail mail" because it travels so much slower than e-mail.

E-mail is like sending a letter except it gets to where it's going in seconds across phone and cable lines. E-mail is delivered almost at the speed of light. But when it is rush hour on the Internet, an e-mail may take a little longer to get wherever it's going.

Instead of a stamp and an address on an envelope, you have an e-mail address in a "header," which is a piece of information sent at the start of your message that tells the computer where it's going and who it's from. Instead of street names and house numbers, e-mail addresses may look like this: pat@anyname.com. It looks weird, but it makes sense when you get used to it. You say it like this: "pat at anyname dot com."

Emails can travel as data on fiber optic cables at nearly the speed of light.

If you or your family has an ISP account, you almost certainly have access to e-mail. If not, you can easily get a free e-mail account. It is probably a good idea for you to have a separate account from anyone else in your family with your own disguised name and password. This way, you or your parents can make the sign-up information secret or in code, so that no tricky person can find out who you are or where you live.

Your e-mail name cannot be a name someone else has already chosen. So, your chances of being just pat@. . . or chris@. . . are just about zero.

But remember, you don't want to choose any name that might give a clue to who you really are anyway. It's also not a good idea to choose a name that will be embarrassing to have on your e-mail. You should talk over your account name with your parents or guardians just to be on the safe side.

It is a federal crime to tamper with the mail, but e-mail can be easily read by more than the sender and the recipient.

CHOOSING A PASSWORD

You will need to choose a password for your e-mail account also. This is so only you can log in, or get access to, your e-mail. Share this password with your parents only. Choose a password that you will be able to remember but that other people using the Internet won't be able to guess.

When you type your password in, it appears as a row of dots or stars, like this: ******

That's so anyone looking over your shoulder can't see what you've typed. Never, never give anyone, even a close friend, your password. They might accidently tell it or write it to the wrong kind of person.

Just as you tell your parents where you are going when you leave your home, they should always know where you are traveling in cyberspace.

SENDING E-MAIL

There are different kinds of e-mail programs out there. They are all set up in similar ways. Some e-mail programs are included with your web browser. You probably would access these programs in the Start menu of your Windows PC and under the Apple menu on Macs. Take a look at a typical e-mail program window. There will be a "new message" button on your e-mail program. Click that to open an new message window. It will look something like this:

E-mails are a lot like writing regular letters, except they travel much faster than the standard mail does.

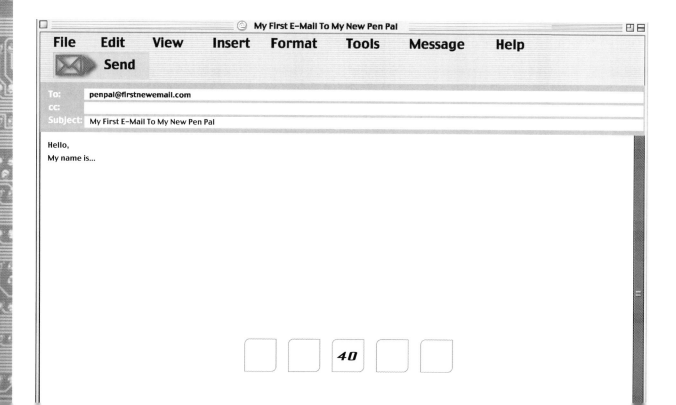

You need to know someone's e-mail address before you can send them a message. Ask friends for their e-mail addresses. E-mail addresses aren't always easy to remember, but luckily you don't have to remember them! In e-mail programs there is an address book that you can find in the program's menu. Type your friends' addresses into your address book. Then, when you want to send a message, you just pick your friend's e-mail name from a list and the e-mail program will open a new message window with your friend's address already in the address line.

Never give anyone's e-mail address out without their permission and never give e-mail addresses to strangers. Never forward someone's e-mail without first taking out their address or any personal information that might be in their message.

Techno Tip

You can send a message to more than one person at a time. Just put all the addresses in the '"To" -line of your mail program. Put commas or semicolons between them and soon your message will be winging its way to all your friends.

If you are sending a message to one person and want someone else to see it, put the second person's address in the "CC" line, or '"copy to" line. You will usually find it under the subject line.

ATTACHING FILES TO YOUR E-MAIL

You can send some extra bits and pieces along with your e-mail. These are called "attachments" or "enclosures" and can be other pieces of work you have done on your computer. For example, you may want to send the map or sound file that you downloaded earlier.

Look for a button on your e-mail program that is labeled "Attachments." It sometimes will have an icon that looks like a paper clip to show that you are clipping something to your mail. Click this Attachments button or icon. A window will pop up with a list of locations on your computer. Choose from the list the place on your computer where you have put the attachment you want to send. Choose the art or sound file. It's attached! Now all you have to do is click "Send." The mail program will dial up the Internet and your mail and attachment will be on their way.

Techno Tip

Watch the size of your attachments! If you attach large files, you will cause all sorts of grief to the people you're sending messages to. Many e-mail services have file size limits. Try not to send files over 50k in size. Also, never send anything over the Internet you wouldn't want your parents, someone else's parents, or a teacher to see.

YOU'VE GOT MAIL!

If you send someone an e-mail, they'll probably send you one back. In your e-mail program's menu you have an "Inbox" button to click on or a "Check Mail" choice. Click or choose these to see if you have any messages. Then click on a message or a "View" button to open your mail and read it.

If you want to send an answer, look for a "Reply" button. You won't need to type in the person's e-mail address. The "reply" feature will address your reply to your friend for you. All you have to do is type in your response to your friend's message and click "Send."

Got no mail? Don't worry. You can find an e-mail pen pal to write to. It can be someone in your own country, or someone on the other side of the world. It's cheaper and quicker than sending regular mail to a kid in a foreign country and even more fun.

E-mail messages with large attachments are like bulky packages: they take up more space and take longer to deliver.

SENDING ONLINE CARDS AND POSTCARDS

Many different places in the cybercity, like museums and zoos, offer online postcards and greeting cards that you can send to friends and family. Visit the San Diego Zoo website and send your mom a postcard to tell her where you've been.

The Internet's potential and capabilities are almost as unlimited as your own.

It's fun getting birthday cards, but don't they all pretty much look the same? What if you could send a card that plays music and and has moving pictures? Some websites allow you to send free cards with pictures and animations. You just have to fill out the address, message, and return address line and your card is on its way. Be sure you don't give out any personal information on this or any other commercial card site.

CYBERSMARTS REVISITED

The Cybercity offers so many great places of interest. So much is happening online that is exciting. All kinds of people use the Internet. There are millions of nice people doing great things with the Internet. But there are also some tricky people using the Internet. Some of them want to scare or hurt kids.

But you can avoid the creepies and have a great time on the Internet and Web if you follow the Cybersmarts Never Rules for traveling online. You may want to write down a list of safety rules that you agree on with your family. These can be a contract, or an understanding, with your family that you come to and sign. It will list how to use the Internet and Web safely. Keep it posted by your computer.

In short, keep your cybersmarts firmly on, use your common sense, and be a responsible citizen of the biggest city on the planet!

Techno Tip

Now that you are sending and receiving mail, you'll want to watch your "Netiquette." That is the Internet way of saying, "Watch your manners and be thoughtful of others."

You'll want to practice good manners on the Internet, because if you don't, you may find that no one will want to talk to you online. Some online services and ISPs have rules about behavior.

When typing, avoid using all caps. TYPING IN CAPS means you are shouting. So, please, hold down your voice and keep your finger off the "Caps lock" key.

Don't use bad language when you are online. Not only will people avoid you, but you could get banned by your Internet service.

Glossary

browser — A program window that allows a user access to the World Wide Web.

hardware — Computers and other machines.

interface — A window on a computer that has menu buttons for opening computer programs.

online — Any activity on the Internet.

search engine — Online tool that helps you move around the Web and find what you are looking for.

servers — Computers that are able to store large amounts of information.

software — Programs and programming languages that run on computers and computer networks.

Further Information

INTERNET SITES

Cybersleuth Kids Search Engine: *http://cybersleuth-kids.com/*

Internet for Kids: *http://www.internet4kids.com/*

Kids Domain: *http://www.kidsdomain.com/*

Kidscom: *http://www.kidscom.com/*

Living Internet: *http://www.livinginternet.com/*

NASA Home Page: *http://www.nasa.gov/*

Safe Kids: *http://www.safekids.com/*

Web Wise Kids: *http://www.webwisekids.com/*

World Kids Network: *http://worldkids.net/*

Index